Naked mole rat teeth never stop growing.

Vultures can soar for hours on the air, rarely flapping their broad wings.

A hummingbird egg is the size of a jelly bean.

Sand tiger shark pups are 3 feet long at birth. This is equivalent to the length of a 4-year-old child.

Jellyfish have been on the earth for 650 million years—400 million years before the first dinosaurs.

Octopi have a beak like a bird.

Panamanian golden frogs' skin poisons come from their diet.

This book is dedicated to all my animal friends:
Esther Museum, Budgie, Magpie, Jack, Fluffy, Pineapple,
Emily, Brownie, and Mr. Bumble.

A very special thanks to Morgan Denney, aquarist, at the National Aquarium in Baltimore, Maryland, for a fascinating behind-the-scenes tour and amazing photography opportunity.

And to my editor, Christy Ottaviano, for her patience and wisdom.

Morgan Denney
Aquarist Extraordinaire

Henry Holt and Company, LLC
Publishers since 1866
175 Fifth Avenue
New York, New York 10010
mackids.com

Henry Holt® is a registered trademark of Henry Holt and Company, LLC.
Copyright © 2015 by Jessica Loy
All rights reserved.

Library of Congress Cataloging-in-Publication Data
Loy, Jessica, author.
Weird & wild animal facts / Jessica Loy. — First edition.
pages   cm
Summary: "There are plenty of books about unusual animals. This is a book about fourteen well-known animals—kangaroos, hippos, giraffes—who all have unusual characteristics. For instance, did you know that a kangaroo's kick can be deadly, that a giraffe can clean its own ears with its tongue, or that a hippo has teeth as long as a child's arm? This accessible book, full of amazing photographs and easy-to-digest factoids, is perfect for animal lovers of all ages."—Provided by publisher
Audience: Ages 4–8.
ISBN 978-0-8050-7945-6 (hardcover)
1. Animals—Miscellanea—Juvenile literature. 2. Children's questions and answers. I. Title. II. Title: Weird and wild animal facts.
QL49.L93 2015   590.2—dc23   2014021236

Henry Holt books may be purchased for business or promotional use. For information on bulk purchases, please contact Macmillan Corporate and Premium Sales Department at (800) 221-7945 x5442 or by e-mail at specialmarkets@macmillan.com.

First Edition—2015

Printed in China by Macmillan Production (Asia) Ltd., Kowloon Bay, Hong Kong (vendor code: 10)

10 9 8 7 6 5 4 3 2 1

Photograph Credits:

All photographs by Jessica Loy, except on the following pages: 10, 23 (upper left), Creative Commons; jacket/case (flamingo, kangaroo, octopus, giraffe's tongue), 13 (upper right), 14 (upper, lower left), 17 (lower left), 22 (center right), 23 (upper right), 28 (bottom left, bottom right), 29 (top left, top right, bottom left), 30 (bottom left), 31 (top), 32 (center right), 33 (top), 34 (top), 35, Shutterstock.com; 14 (lower right), 15, Veer; 18 (top left), University of Illinois at Chicago, Photography; 28 (upper left), Snakecollector/flickr.com/photos/8373783@N07/3200539228; 29 (bottom right), RSW Photography.
Photographs by Jessica Loy were taken at the following locations: Maryland Zoo, Baltimore, MD; National Aquarium, Baltimore, MD; Philadelphia Zoo, Philadelphia, PA; Saint Louis Zoo, St. Louis, MO; Southwick's Zoo, Mendon, MA; Wildlife Conservation Society's Bronx Zoo, Bronx, NY.

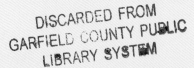

WEiRD
& WiLD
ANIMAL
FACTS

JESSICA LOY

Christy Ottaviano Books
Henry Holt and Company
New York

Contents

Giant Pacific Octopus 8

Giraffe **10**

Hippopotamus **12**

Hummingbird 14

Jellyfish 16

Naked Mole Rat 18

Panamanian Golden Frog 20

Red Kangaroo **22**

Sand Tiger Shark 24

Sea Horse 26

Tarantula 28

Two-Toed Sloth **30**

Vulture 32

Warthog 34

More Fun Facts **36**

Introduction

The natural world holds amazing secrets and contains many strange and exotic-looking creatures. But in my search for unusual animal characteristics, I learned that some of the most common animals have very uncommon attributes. These remarkable adaptations aid in such things as hunting, self-defense, and communication. Did you know a hummingbird can fly backward or that the Panamanian golden frog has no ears? Some animals have characteristics scientists don't even fully understand yet.

I selected the fourteen animals in this book because many are familiar to us, yet have unexpected talents. So take a peek inside, learn some fun facts, and share them with your friends and family.

Do you have a special talent?

Giant Pacific Octopus

Octopi are intelligent. They can process complex information, and they have an excellent memory.

Octopi can't see color, but they change their appearance to match the texture, contrast, and brightness of their surroundings, making them **invisible** to predators and prey.

Octopus Eye

The **suction cups** are probably more important to an octopus than their eyes. Each suction cup can be controlled individually, like human **fingers**, and is equipped with chemical receptors, so that the octopus can **taste** what it is handling.

Octopi have a beak like a
bird, which they use to eat shellfish.

Beak

Females lay up to 90,000 eggs
in a den, and stay with them until they hatch.
During this time the mother stops eating.
She dies soon after the eggs hatch.

Giraffe

Giraffes can grow up to **18 feet tall,** making them the tallest land mammals in the world.

A giraffe can clean its ears with its **21-inch tongue.** That's longer than a loaf of bread.

A giraffe's tongue is **black.**

An
adult giraffe's
kick is
so powerful
it can **decapitate
a lion.**

kick

Giraffe **spots are
unique** to each animal
just like human fingerprints.

Giraffes can
run up to
**35 miles
per hour.**

Hippopotamus

Hippos secrete a thick red substance called **blood sweat,** which protects them from sunburns.

Hippos can hold their breath for five minutes walking **along the bottom** of a lake or river.

A hippo's ears, eyes, and nose are **all on top of its head** so it can watch its surroundings while in the water.

Hippos **open their mouths** as wide as possible to size each other up. Their canine teeth can grow to 20 inches long—about the length of a child's arms.

Hippos are among the **most dangerous** and aggressive of all mammals. Since they are vegetarians, their bad temper is defensive only.

Fish clean the hippo's skin by **eating algae** that collects on it.

A hummingbird's **wings rotate 360 degrees** so it can fly up, down, sideways, forward, backward, or stand still in the air.

Rufous Hummingbird

Humming-bird

A hummingbird nest is the size of a **Ping-Pong ball**, and a hummingbird egg is the size of a **jelly bean**.

Rufous Hummingbird

Allen's Hummingbird

The shimmering colors of a hummingbird come from something called iridescence. Color appears to change as light is refracted by certain feather structures and the angle of the viewer.

Male Ruby-Throated Hummingbird

Actual Size

A penny is heavier than a hummingbird.

A hummingbird's heart can beat up to 1,260 times per minute. The human heart beats an average of 92 times per minute.

Female Ruby-Throated Hummingbird

15

Jellyfish

Northern
Sea Nettle →

A jellyfish's body
is 95% water.

Jellyfish have been on the
earth for 650 million
years—400 million years
before the first dinosaurs.
They live in every ocean in
the world, in the shallows
and the farthest depths of
the ocean. There are over
2,000 known species.

↑
Spotted Lagoon Jelly

Moon Jelly →

Jellyfish have
no brain,
no respiratory system,
no circulatory system,
and no excretory system.

Jellyfish **never stop** growing. Some jellyfish are smaller than an inch and others are larger than 7 feet, with tentacles that extend over 100 feet.

Purple Striped Jelly

Pacific Sea Nettle

Most jellyfish sting. The stinging cells, called nematocysts, are located in their tentacles and **release venom** when they come in contact with an apparent threat. The tentacles remain attached to the skin of the victim. Even a dead jellyfish can sting.

Box Jellyfish

One box jellyfish has enough **venom** to kill 60 people and is the most dangerous of all sea creatures to humans.

Naked

Mole rats can see only light and shadow, so they **use their whiskers** to feel along dark burrows.

They can **run backward** and forward equally fast. This is quite unusual in mammals.

Naked mole rats **are like bees.** Every member of the colony has a specific job. There are breeders, housekeepers, soldiers, and a queen. When a new queen takes over, her body gets longer.

Mole Rat

Naked mole rat teeth **never stop growing.** This allows them to dig without wearing their teeth down.

Naked mole rat colonies create **toilet chambers.** When one is full, they seal it up and make a new one.

Naked mole rats live underground in burrows. Their mazes can be equal to 20 football fields.

The Panamanian golden frog, like all frogs, has no true teeth.

Panamanian Golden Frog

◀ Ants ▶

Panamanian golden frogs' skin poisons come from their diet of insects, especially ants, which contain formic acid.

Scientists have found that one Panamanian golden frog contains enough toxins to kill 1,200 mice.

Panamanian golden frogs have no external ears! It's thought they detect sound through their lungs, which are directly under the skin and vibrate when sound waves hit them.

Red Kangaroo

A newborn kangaroo, which is **smaller than a cherry**, climbs into its mother's pouch soon after birth. Two months later, it will begin to spend time outside the pouch.

A female kangaroo is called **a flyer**. The male is **a boomer**. A baby is called **a joey**, and a group of kangaroos is called **a mob**.

Kangaroos can balance on their **strong tails,** allowing them to fight with their feet.

A red kangaroo can leap 25 feet across and **10 feet high** in a single jump and can reach speeds of 35 miles per hour.

On land a kangaroo's **hind legs can only** move together in a hop. But while swimming, they kick each leg independently.

Kangaroos have **five fingers** on each hand, like humans.

Sand Tiger

Sand tiger sharks can have more than 3,000 teeth and on average lose 1,000 teeth per year. The teeth are arranged in rows, and a new tooth will move up to take a lost one's place. This ensures their teeth are always sharp.

Sand shark pups are 3 feet long at birth. This is about the size of a 4-year-old child.

Shark

Sharks adjust their buoyancy by gulping air at the surface and then burping. This strategy allows them to hover almost motionless in the water.

"Excuse me!"

Sand tiger sharks are the only known sharks that surface to take in air.

These sharks look ferocious but are actually quite docile.

Sea Horse

Sea horses have **no teeth.** They use their tubelike mouths to create **a vacuum** that sucks up small shrimp and other prey.

Sea horses have eyes **like a lizard.** Each eye moves independent of the other.

All sea horses swim **while upright.**

Leafy Sea Dragon

A close relative of
the sea horse is the exotic-looking
leafy sea dragon.

Baby Sea Horses

Baby sea horses are carried
by the **males,** not the females.
Males are pregnant for three
weeks and give birth to as many
as **200 young** at a time.

To hide from predators,
sea horses can **change
their color** to blend in
with the environment.

27

Tarantula

Goliath Tarantula

The largest tarantulas have a leg span of **nearly 10 inches,** or about the size of a dinner plate.

Tarantulas **have fangs** to attack their prey.

Red Knee Tarantula

A female tarantula lays **500 to 1,000 eggs** in a silken sac, which she guards until they hatch 6 to 7 weeks later.

Tarantulas inject their prey with paralyzing venom, then use digestive enzymes to **melt their victim's** body into soup, which they drink through their straw-like mouth.

Golden Brown Baboon Tarantula

Most tarantulas **live underground** in burrows.

Arizona Blond Tarantula

Tarantulas have retractable claws, **just like cats,** which they use to grip.

Two-Toed Sloth

Sloths can **go days without eating,** and they defecate only once a week. They descend to the ground where they dig a hole to use as a **toilet.** Their back legs are not very strong, so they must drag themselves along the forest floor with their arms.

Sloths are covered in unique **fur** that's an ideal breeding ground for algae. The **algae helps them** blend into the environment and hide from **predators.**

Anteater

Sloths are related to **anteaters.**

Sloth mothers give birth to **one** baby per year.

Sloths are the **slowest mammals** on earth, and climb upside down through tree branches. They are **arboreal** creatures, which means they live in trees.

Sloths sleep as much as **15 to 18 hours a day.**

The sloth's long claws are **good for gripping** branches and are their only natural defense.

Vulture

A group of flying vultures is
called **a kettle**.

European
Griffon Vulture

Lappet-faced Vulture

Vultures specialize in eating
animals that are **already
dead.** They prevent the spread
of dangerous diseases such as
rabies by consuming the
carcasses of diseased animals.

They can **survive diseases**
that would kill any other creature,
including humans.

Vultures can **soar for hours** on the air, rarely flapping their broad wings.

Many vultures have **bald heads,** which means there are no feathers to **clean** after sticking their heads inside the carcass of a dead animal.

King Vulture

Cinereous Vulture

Vultures **urinate on their legs** to kill germs they might pick up while feeding on a carcass. They also use this technique **to cool off** because birds do not have sweat glands.

Warthog

Warthogs have **four tusks**, two on either side of their face, which they use for defense or to dig for bulbs and other food.

These animals **roam** in small groups called **sounders**.

Juvenile Warthogs

34

← knee pad

Since warthogs
eat and drink kneeling,
they have developed
knee pads
made of callused
skin patches to
protect themselves.

Warthogs are named
for the **warts** on
their face.

Like horses, warthogs
have **manes.**

Warthogs run
with their tails straight
in the air and can run up
to **30 miles per hour.**

More Fun Facts

Elephant

A flamingo's vibrant pink color comes from eating beta carotene–rich algae and shrimp.

Flamingo

The elephant is one of several mammals that can't jump.

Lemurs travel in groups called troops.

Lemur

Tortoise

Each rhino's odor is unique. They use piles of dung to leave messages for other rhinos.

Rhinoceros

A porcupine's quills are hollow, which gives them their bouyancy in water.

Porcupine

A tortoise's shell is not a separate house but part of its body's skeleton.

Resources

Association of Zoos and
Aquariums

aza.org/findzooaquarium

Bronx Zoo and Wildlife
Conservation Society

Bronx, NY

bronxzoo.com/animals-and-exhibits.aspx

Maryland Zoo

Baltimore, MD

marylandzoo.org/animals-conservation/mammals

National Aquarium

Baltimore, MD

aqua.org

National Audubon Society

birds.audubon.org/birds

National Geographic

animals.nationalgeographic.com/animals

New England Aquarium

Boston, MA

neaq.org/animals_and_exhibits

Oregon Zoo

Portland, OR

oregonzoo.org

Philadelphia Zoo

Philadelphia, PA

philadelphiazoo.org/Animals.htm

Pittsburgh Zoo

Pittsburgh, PA

pittsburghzoo.org/AnimalsandExhibits

Saint Louis Zoo

St. Louis, MO

stlzoo.org/animals/abouttheanimals

Scientific American

scientificamerican.com

Southwick's Zoo

Mendon, MA

southwickszoo.com

Sloths can go days without eating.

Warthogs have a mane like a horse.

Kangaroos can balance on their strong tails.

Sea horses can change their color.

Hippos can hold their breath underwater for five minutes.

Tarantulas have fangs.

Giraffes are the tallest land mammals in the world.